Light and Dark

Jarred Marsh

Light and Dark

Copyright © 2024 by Jarred Marsh.

All rights reserved. No part of this book may be reproduced in any form or by any electronic or mechanical means, including information storage and retrieval systems, without permission in writing from the publisher, except by reviewers, who may quote brief passages in a review.

This publication contains the opinions and ideas of its author. It is intended to provide helpful and informative material on the subjects addressed in the publication. The author and publisher specifically disclaim all responsibility for any liability, loss, or risk, personal or otherwise, which is incurred as a consequence, directly or indirectly, of the use and application of any of the contents of this book.

MILTON & HUGO L.L.C.
4407 Park Ave., Suite 5
Union City, NJ 07087, USA

Website: *www. miltonandhugo.com*
Hotline: *1- 888-778-0033*
Email: *info@miltonandhugo.com*

Ordering Information:
Quantity sales. Special discounts are available on quantity purchases by corporations, associations, and others. For details, contact the publisher at the address above.

Library of Congress Control Number:	2024911969
ISBN-13: 979-8-89285-194-7	[Paperback Edition]
979-8-89285-193-0	[Digital Edition]

Rev. date: 06/04/2024

The Summer Flowers

Freshly bloomed
Boundlessly sweet
No matter where you are
I wish you well.
To grow and blossom
To inspire and amaze.

By the riverbeds and ponds
In the hills and mountains
Wherever you land and
Whatever you go through
I'll always be rooting you on.

When your petals start to fall
When you feel weak and hopeless
When all seems faded and lost
The earth and sun will claim you
Until you are once again
Freshly bloomed and boundlessly sweet.

Valhalla Calls

Valhalla calls for me. It is not time for me to answer yet though. It is comforting to know that I will have a seat amongst the finest when I am ready. Death will smile with greed and joy as I litter the fields. The Valkyrie will be as busy as bees as I set foot into the midst of battle. Swords will sing, arrows will whistle, shields will drum the baseline, and all those who have braved the field that day will chant their people's words. From shore to shore, my legend will grow. May the wind be harsh and the currents strong so that we don't grow weak and lazy. May our bellies be full and our hearts glowing so that we fight happily. Till death finally catches us, may we fight and laugh and love to the fullest of which we are capable.

Love

I have yet to understand why. I try not to ask and just accept it as the gift it is. I never feel deserving of it. Yet there it is, unwavering and steady. Always there to guide me when I've strayed off path. Always there when I need it. Always ready to comfort me. I try and try to do better for it. Not because I'm expected to, but because I want to. I want it to know that I care and want to do better in my life so that when it needs me, I can provide the same strength that it has given to me.

Now what is it, you may wonder.

That's simple. It's you.

A Cycle of Beauty

The flowers bloom, and the birds sing

The sun rises, and the sun sets

Any person can see such things, can they not?

Her beauty lights up a room

Her energy livens everyone's mood

How can everyone see that except for her?

I see her strength as she supports those around her

I see her kindness as she shares laughter with all

How can someone be so perfect and still be human?

She calls herself so many negative names, but I never see it

Why is her mind so cruel to her to not even accept its own beauty?

If only she could see herself through my eyes just once

If only she could hear the praise and compliments that people whisper of her

Maybe then she could see herself the way I do

I sing her praise, I shout of her beauty to the tops of the roofs

I clown and joke just to see her smile or hear her laugh

I hope today is the day that she can see

Just as the sun sets and rises, she is essential in the lives of so many

Just as the birds sing and flowers bloom, her beauty is a gift to all

Any person can see such things, can they not?

All That Is on My Mind

I sit and stare at the ceiling for hours after I awake. I ponder all the things that have been and all the things that will come. My mind never wants to rest. Always racing from one idea and thought to the next. I find that no matter where my mind goes, it always comes back to you. Even if just for a moment before racing off again, you are always on my mind.

Nothing is more beautiful to me than you. Like the snow-covered mountains we once played in. Like the blue sky we once flew through. Like the gentle crashing of the waves on a sandy beach in the cold winter months. Like the blissful chirping of all the critters late at night where the moon shines bright and the stars fill the air.

My memories are filled with you. Our goofy adventures, silly ideas, and the things that seem so mundane but were so exciting because I had you. The late-night adventures to go to the grocery store, or the random dates to go sit in a fast-food place just to be together for a bit. The adventures across the country and the adventures of doing nothing. The exciting times of going to weddings, and the exciting times of waking up late and rushing off to class or work. I look back at all of these things and feel the same warmth. The same happiness that you have brought me day after day.

The Noise of the World

This world never stops with the chatter. Silence is such a rarity. My greatest joy in this life has been the brief moments when my gaze met hers and I no longer heard any of the world's noise. Even if I had, it didn't matter. My own world was at peace and in silence as I looked on. My only wish is that things could stay like that forever. But alas, she doesn't even know me. And the world will always continue to chatter.

As the weeks go by, my goal is simple: silence the world as much as possible. To hear her laugh or to see her blush is incredible. My heart races. I don't mind talking to her. Maybe not all the chatter in the world is bad. Maybe listening to her is as good as my silence.

End of an Angel

Summer flowers on her deathbed

A small crown fitted around her head

She died today, and my eyes filled with sorrow

I wonder what could have been for us tomorrow

Her expression sat blank

Such a contrast from what I was used to be frank

Her joyous smile

Has been void for a while

Forevermore, may she be my angel of death, to watch over my every breath.

I See You, Always

Around every corner, I see you. In every shape, I dream a piece of you. I wonder where you would be today. How many more hearts you would have touched. How many more smiles you would have brought to those around you. What sorts of trouble you would be poking in. It's amazing that even though you aren't here anymore, I still see you everywhere.

Mindless

I lost my mind today. I'm not quite sure where though. I hope whoever picks it up is happy with it. It served me well for many years, both through the highs and lows, the good and bad, happy and sad. I wonder what they will do with it, if they will satisfy its thirst for knowledge. If they will train it to be a sharp tool, or if they will have it simply to say they have one. Maybe a collector will find it and add it to their collection. Or perhaps they will destroy it for fear of what it may be. I cannot say what the fate of my mind will be, nor do I know what my own fate will be now. I already feel the void tugging my soul away from my body. It's likely that I will become a shell to aimlessly wander until my earthly body dies. My thoughts bounce around in this empty head. This would be a good spot to make bed. Perhaps I will luck out and find a new mind. Better make sure there's nothing coming up from behind. Maybe the next one will be the one that has the cure to cancer or the key to world peace. I'd be happy if it had enough reason to teach me how to love myself. I think I'd make a pretty good elf. Maybe then I wouldn't lose any more of my minds. Ha-ha, girls' behinds. Hehe. Oh right, my mind. Where are you off to now? Exit stage right after you've taken your bow. And a merry good-night to one and all, said the shell.

A Grand Adventure

Every day, I stray farther from my intended path. I've searched far and wide, but nothing ever catches the eye. I had hoped for such great adventures. Now, my only hope is to survive. My tale may not be glorious. It may not be grand. There may not even be a happy ending, as fate seems to love a good tragedy. However, at the end of each day, and at the end of each adventure it is still my story. I am still in charge of this vessel. No matter how loud the void calls my name or how far I go off path, I will hold my head as high as I can each day. I will fight with every ounce of strength I have in my body. I will love with every passion and fiber I have in my heart. I will give my everything each day until I am finished. I will carry my physical, mental, and emotional scars as badges of honor. A simple proof that whatever tried to defeat me was unsuccessful—that I was the tougher one that day. For the sake of those around me, I will push onward. I am no knight in shiny armor. No, my metal and mettle have been tested time and time again. I am no hero. I have hurt those around me and am likely the villain in others' stories. To those I have hurt, I hope they forgive me. I strive each day to grow stronger and wiser. I grow so that whenever those around me fall, I may have the strength to pick them up. I have depended on so many to get to where I am today. It's my turn to give some light back to this world. And I intend to shine brighter than the sun itself.

To Love and Lose

We have all lost someone whom we loved and cherished. Yet no one ever truly understands the pain you feel from that. No one shared the same bond you had with them, so how could they even fathom how it pains you? How my heart feels broken so deeply that I'm concerned for the strength of my soul. No one realizes how deeply it cuts. The times when I cry aloud until I can't breathe. The times I fake a smile and move forward despite the pain flowing constantly and slowly, like blood from an unstitched wound.

I wanted to be selfish. To have one more moment. To have the chance for one more hug. To be able to say "I love you" and hear you say it back one more time. I want to curse, cry, and scream. I want to blame anyone for taking you away. I want to see your face one last time. Not just the pictures or the videos. I want one more holiday. One more special moment. One more mundane moment. One opportunity to say how much you mean to me. How I loved you so dearly. How my life will never be the same without you.

Ironically, I'm envious. How peaceful it must be. For there to never be another tomorrow. Never another fear. Never another worry. Never another sickness. Never another sad thought. Only the warmth of the sun and grass covering what's left of you. To be at peace finally.

Any time your existence may be rekindled in someone's mind, no matter how bad the memory, there will always be a hint of happiness in there. Because you are in that memory. Because you are special. I wish I could've stolen your pain. I wish that anyone who remembers you remembers you at your best. I wish that they only remember the good you did. Though my heart is broken, I smile for you were in my life. I move through the pain because you live within my mind. I hope one day I will see you again. I hope one day, my selfish dreams come true as

I get to tell you all the things I didn't get to here. I hope, if nothing else, that I can tell you one last time that I love you.

Peeling Flesh

Losing someone special can be a lot like peeling dying flesh. It's painful as it grips so tightly to you. The immediate pain may be unbearable and unimaginable for others to perceive. The scars left behind will be a constant reminder of how great things once were and how they will never be the same again. Let these memories comfort you. For with time, the pain subsides. Remind yourself that at least the pain and suffering has lessened.

Lost

I meant what I said when I said it. But everything has changed since then. I walked my path, and you walked yours. The two were never fated to intertwine. I bent over backwards to do this and that for you. Went above and beyond and out of my way for you. While you only ever tried when it was convenient for you. You said you cared, but I never felt it. I tried and tried. I don't know if you didn't notice or just didn't care, but I guess that doesn't really matter. I lost countless hours of sleep just trying to buy time to make the connections. So many sleepless days and nights just to learn it was a waste of time.

I Hate Myself for Loving You

I would have moved mountains, committed atrocities, or saved humanity from its self-destruction for you. All I wanted was to gaze but a moment longer into your soul. There was no reason for my love, but it was instant. It made no sense to love you, but you filled my mind like books in a library. I barely knew you, yet you were my everything. I hate myself for loving you.

I yearn for a sensation of sorts that allows me to put you at fault. You came into my life with the same ease as the sun rising, and you were gone with haste just as the sun setting. I hate myself for loving you.

You did no wrong to me. It was I who fell into undeniable insanity over you. You are a perfect being in my eyes. The only angel to ever exist on this planet. A goddess amongst all. I hate myself for loving you.

It was I that held you upon the pedestal. It was I that felt your presence with the same warmth as the sun. It was I who fell in an endless void when you disappeared. It was I who is to blame for my love to you. I hate myself for loving you.

Life moves on. The sun rises, bringing in all of its light and warmth. The sun sets, fleeing the sky like a cold void. I hold my truths of who you are. My heart gets broken as you continue down your path. With tape and glue, I'll piece myself together without you. I hate myself for loving you.

The Masks of Life

I wake up each day and choose my mask. Some days, I choose the jovial mask. Other days, I chose the jocular mask. I have other masks in my arsenal, but these two are my favorite. They lead those around me to believe that all is well and everything is okay. It allows me to be a shining inspiration, a shoulder to lean on, or someone who can lighten a room with humor without anyone ever truly knowing what goes on behind these eyes. The more I wear the masks, the heavier they get. The harder it becomes to tell what is real and what's fake. I question at times if I will lose myself or my sanity behind these masks. At first, the masks were created for emergencies and rare occasions. Now, I find myself dependent on them daily. I ponder if I've gone too far. This is how everyone expects me to be now. The masked one. I will be okay as long as no one ever sees through the cracks of my disguise.

Afraid of the Day

Afraid of the dark? No. I fear no honorable creature. The cryptids and creatures who hide in the shadows of the night must first show themselves before they can harm you. They must reveal themselves from the dark and show their intentions. What you should fear are the demons who walk in broad daylight. Those who blend in perfectly without ever raising any alarms in you. Those are the ones who will torture and eat you alive. Those beasts will call you friend or pal, but the minute your back is turned, you're nothing but a game to them. Those are the beast that scare me, surrounding me on all sides and at every turn. I fear the day because I never know which person will finally be the one to end me.

I Sit and Stare into the Darkness

Unsure whether I'd feel more fear if something looked back at me or if the darkness was simply unending.

The fire that once burned so brightly in my heart is no more.

The day-to-day processes of life, the mere being of but a cog in the machine of life has finally drained all hopes and dreams from my body.

At every turn, I hoped I was rallying to my peak.

Yet nothing more ever developed.

Each moment of truth led only to a crumbling failure or a mundane splash of water to wake me back to this reality.

At the edge of my bed, could this truly be all life is meant to be?

Another moment will pass by, aimless as ever, as I sit and stare into the darkness.

A Final Moment

Surrounded by darkness. I don't know where I am. I hear a woman crying in the distance. It feels like I am being held. How nice her warm embrace is. The scent of her perfume creeps into my nostrils, like a sweet citrus drink at the beach. I am so warm. So numb. The last thing I remember is a loud bang. The feeling of her touch is starting to fade. Her voice becomes harder and harder to hear. Is this the last time I will ever feel her warmth? Is this the last time I will ever be able to experience happiness? Never to see her or to hear her laugh again? How selfish it was of me to never realize these joys, but I suppose that this is the punishment of death.

Lady Death

I often dream and think of death in all her beauty as she gently carries people away. Away from their suffering, away from this sick and dying world. She takes them away from the pain and hate that so prominently fills the world. Yet people fear her grace and shun her. I don't understand why so many fear death when they have yet to even begin to live. They will run, hide, and beg for more time. They should instead welcome her and thank her. Tell her of their victories, the hardships they overcame, the loves they enjoyed, the success they found at every corner. It's so rare to have the opportunity to be cared for unconditionally and carried away. You may as well enjoy it; she will pick us all up one day.

Jimmy Eats the Rich

It's time to leave this place.
They'll only spit on your face.
Time to walk down the streets alone
Begging anyone for their phone.
I don't know what I'm looking for.
I'd settle for anything more…
More than this dirt taste in my mouth.
More than this hate I feel in my skin.
More than this rage in my bones.
They say money won't buy you happiness
But they sure looked happier to me through the glass pane door.
I just want a taste of it.
I just want a feel for it.
It all turns to red.
Bodies mangled everywhere.
I ate until I felt sick.
I ate until I felt rich.
I suffered through the taste of shit, and I did it all for you.
The pigs look down on us and take advantage of our every move.
So I ate them. I ate them all.
I know this may be my last day with y'all.
The cops will surely show.
These folks were worth more than just the shirt on their backs, ya know?
They'll bust down the door and say, "Jimmy, put your hands in the air."

"Jimmy, don't move a single muscle, what you've done just ain't fair."

"Jimmy, how could you do this to these families? Don't you care?"

I'll put my hands behind my back.

I'll tell them I'm not going with them to the shack.

When they get close…

I'll point my finger guns at 'em.

And they'll take me out for good.

And they'll take me out for good…

They'll split open my mind with a bullet of justice for my enlightenment.

They'll open my eyes to my own masterpiece.

Scatter my brain in a beautiful pattern across the wall.

A modern-day Mona Lisa.

A masterpiece even Da Vinci could not replicate.

I ate the rich people for you.

I ate them to leave the world in a more beautiful form than when I found it.

Finally, my life's art is complete.

Midnight Murder

There was something lurking in the halls. Something that made my eyes feel like static as I tried to look at it. The longer I stared, the blurrier it became. My throat felt like sandpaper with each terrified swallow. I was shivering on the hottest night of the year.

Maybe if I turn away, it will just go somewhere else, right? Then why can I feel my whole body shaking? Why do I feel like a block of ice? I need to get up. I've got to run away. I need to scream to try to wake someone up or do something. I need this stupid body to do anything so I can escape what is surely going to be my doom. I HAVE TO DO IT NOW. I NEED TO GET UP. IF I DON'T MOVE NOW, I'M… I'm…

I'm too late. It's in my room. I can feel it standing over me. There's no mistaking that feeling. Its presence is so intense, yet it's so quiet. I can't hear anything over the sound of my own panicked breath and pounding heart. I wonder if it will be painful. I wonder if my parents will be traumatized by the carnage left behind. Every ounce of my body wants to turn so I can at least see this creature. So I may at least know what is going to be the end of me. This is strange. I know it was here. I know in not crazy. Yet I don't see anything. I'm no longer shaking or cold. Could it have been my imagination? What a cruel trick that would have been for my brain to play on my heart. Perhaps I should just go back to sleep then.

The time on the clock reads 12:01. This monster fiasco began almost three hours ago. How strange that time has flown by so quickly. I feel as though I'm drained of all energy. This little panic attack has done a serious number to me. I'll rest my eyes for a bit before getting up to eat a snack. I feel like I've tossed and turned for hours, but the clock says 12:02 now. That can't be right. There's no way I've only slept one minute. Unless I've actually slept twenty-four hours? No, surely not.

As I opened my eyes again, I was face-to-face with it. The most horrifying abomination I've ever laid eyes on. Its deerlike antlers were dark and chipped. Its two human faces appeared to be crudely sewn together. One face had both eyes and a nose but no jaw. While the main face had but one eye, and its jaw was split in the middle. The tongue hanging out in between the two pieces was with abnormal length. Its hair was long but in patches. Strangely, its smell was pleasant at this close. Earlier, it had smelt of burning flesh; but now, it was almost like a sweet vanilla. I still couldn't make out what its body looked like. Only static. *Why do I feel at peace now that this thing is so close to me? Is it because I know my death has arrived and there's nothing I can do against it?*

The creature began to chew off chunks of my face. With each bite, it would place the flesh against its own almost, as if trying to fit puzzle pieces together. I wanted to scream. I wanted to run. I wanted someone to save me. But alas, it seemed I would simply sit and suffer.

Wait. Have I not been able to move this whole time? Have I really been numb for this whole process? Oh yeah. This must be my first step of suffering in hell. These two faces kind of look like my parents now that I can focus a bit more. This must be my divine punishment for killing my parents then myself. I had good intentions though. I didn't want the voices to get them. They lurked in the halls every night, calling out their names, begging me to do horrible things to them. Maybe I shouldn't have used a shotgun. Maybe then I could've died a little faster. On the bright side, the voices are finally quiet.

Returning of a King

Suddenly, it stood up. With a step so monumental, it felt as if it shook the very earth we stood on. In reality, it was only our hearts jumping and trembling at this moment. Before us stood a king. No, whatever this creature was has ascended well beyond flesh and bone. What stood before us was surely a god. A god in the eyes of every single being that witnessed it. Despite having yet to say anything, it was clear that this feeling was universal. The being was covered from head to toe in a dull bronzelike metal that clashed and clanged together as it moved. However, it flowed like a silk shirt in the wind. From where the being stood, it seemed that it would tower over even the tallest of humans. Its physique was that of an Olympian; muscled and toned to an extreme measure of near perfection. Once the being finally spoke, its voice was low and raspy, yet no one had difficulty hearing its words. It spoke in a manner that felt transcendent, crystal clear, omnipotent even. It spoke only three words. After years of sitting on this throne in the middle of our city and having never moved at all, it said to us, "Time to slaughter." The energy that pulled us all to the throne that morning had been sweet, like a cool summer breeze inviting you to the shade to cool off. Now the air was stifling and stagnant. A pungent odor surrounded the area. The very air around us felt as though it was trying to strangle us.

The being suddenly crumbled and flaked into a small pile of debris. People began to panic as violence broke out. Hatred filled the minds and hearts of many. It sent them into a frenzy. They attacked everyone around them. No one was safe as mothers attacked their children, brothers struggled against brothers, and neighbors slaughtered each other. The streets of the city turned to red from the rivers of blood that now flowed. A sunny day had turned gray with a fierce storm that seemed to rain so heavily it felt like blood falling. It didn't take long for dead bodies to litter every twist and turn of the city. Skirmishes of a few turned into all-out brawls of many until only one remained.

Maybe I was too weak, and that's why I filled with panic instead of hate. I ran to the nearest house and barricaded myself inside. I watched through a hole in the wall as a mother picked up a child and used it as a weapon, beating what I assume was her other child to death. Relentlessly beating until the head finally tore away from the rest of the infant's body. Her child was mangled with a face smashed beyond any point of recognition. They all three howled as the events unfolded. Perhaps the howl was a curse to the world for such cruelty, or maybe of pure pain that they all felt both physically and emotionally. It was horrific, yet my heart yearned to see more. I wanted more than anything to join the chaos. It was a very primal feeling from deep within the soul.

I began to wonder what exactly that creature was. Was it the Mad King of old? A man born into poverty who became king by ruthlessly destroying entire villages. A king who was elevated to the status of a god by his followers. He was known by friend and foe alike for his cruelty, holding slaughter festivals to help cull populations. The Mad King targeted the poor and people he considered foreigners. As his time of death approached, he rode from city to city, promising an eternal paradise to all those who could survive. All they had to do was kill everyone else. Then he took each of the champions and fed them a sacred meal of human brains. Next, the Mad King himself slaughtered the survivors. Cutting each one for every kill they had made. Their blood-drunk rage caused them to howl in anger, for each cut was deep and long. Surely this couldn't be the work of the Mad King though. He's been dead for over two hundred years after all. He slit his throat here in the middle of our city. On his throne…

Left to Wander

Letting my mind wander through a self-built prison.

Viewing all the dead beings on the floor that once floated as beautiful dreams.

Slipping through the cracks of the walls, questioning if my age is the source of the corruption within.

Searching aimlessly through the broken floor, hopeful to find any crumb of ambition and drive that has long been forgotten.

Running my hand along the dark and dusty ceiling, choking on the filth as it drops around me.

Light dares not show its beauty here.

Has the system poisoned me? Or have my eyes finally adjusted to reality?

My mind wanders deeper into despair.

A Winter Hike

Steam was still rising off his body in the cold air. I love him. I had asked my best friend to join me for a hike in the cold mountains of Colorado. We had been best friends since middle school, watched each other turn into adults. I know how he suffered though. Sometimes, the world is so cruel. I couldn't bear the thought of him suffering anymore. I love him. So, I saved him. I planned for the coldest and windiest day for the hike. My goal was simple, but he would have to suffer a little more before I could help him be at peace. Once we had ventured far enough into the woods to set up camp for the night, I strangled him. He barely put up a fight. I hope that was his way of saying thank-you. I love him after all. I know hiding the body would be the more difficult task to handle now. I wanted to preserve him as he is, but I know he would be harder to find in pieces. I know what needed to be done. Bears roam and attack people all the time in the woods, right? I hated the thought of having to take apart my best friend, but it had to be convincing, right? Everything was going to work out perfectly. I'd dismember the body, bury most of it, grease some up so that bears and wolves would eat it and report the attack when I returned to town in five days. Maybe I should have let us get out farther. What if they'd find him quickly and say I murdered him? I loved him. He's my best friend. I would never do anything as evil as murder. I simply set him free. Someone was approaching. I didn't want to kill an innocent bystander. *Please don't come this way.* I did what I had to do to save my best friend, I love him after all. When the park ranger saw me covered in blood with an axe over a corpse, he opened fire. Now I was the one steaming while my soon-to-be-lifeless body lay on the ground. What a cruel twist! I won't even be able to tell them about how I saved my best friend. Perhaps this is the universe's way of keeping us united? How beautiful. I love him so. Soon, we can hang out together forever and never have to suffer again. Now, I may die happily.

A Setting Sun

How beautiful is the setting sun on rolling hills or a mountaintop? This may be a strange thought to have while lying on a grassy plain surrounded by corpses. Maybe the bloodstained grass triggered a thought of what could be assumed as the orangeish reflection of the sun setting along the horizon. The warmth from the sun would be more present to my front though in that scenario. Whereas the heat here from the body's dance around with no certainty of direction. How did I get here? What aligned so perfectly to lead me to this very moment? I was supposed to graduate college and get some big fancy job. Instead, I find myself lost at every turn, doing mundane tasks for a mass retail bigwig.

Ah yes, I recall now. This man next to me—or rather what's left of him next to me. Had the audacity to tell me that for my life to get better, I simply had to pull myself up by the bootstraps, completely ignoring that his generation was not only holding all of the bootstraps but they also ruined the boot. Maybe thirty-eight times was excessive. Or perhaps in his eyes, I did not meet the expectations of his undeniable vigor in attitude and should therefore continue. I'd hate for him to think I'm just another lazy punk kid that only puts in minimal effort after all. That man down there asked me, "Are you stupid?" Funny, if only he could see his own face now. Then he may understand the enigma and perplexity of my mind. That one way over there barked and demanded that I "get a move on" and "stop being such a waste of space." There are so many around me. It'd be hard to count them all. That is, if I hadn't counted as it happened. There are one hundred and twenty-six. I wonder if there would have been as many if I had been on that beautiful mountaintop. If I had been happier, would this have still been the outcome?

The blood on the grass with such a clear sky creates a contrast of colors that are simply marvelous. Perhaps I'm not the artist that my mother had hoped for, but an artist nonetheless. I'm certainly not creating masterpieces that will be talked about for years even after my own death, like the works of all the renowned Renaissance artist. However, it is my authentic art. I killed them all, I moved their bodies in this arrangement. I created this very scene. Some strokes occurred with joy and glee while others were filled with hate and prejudice.

Every piece of me that tried to stop me from becoming my true self I killed and put down. Unfortunately, now, there isn't much left and that makes me sad. A mere shell rotting away in what was once a grand hall. At least I'm happy now. This warm embrace by the void. The slight tingle that helps me avoid all emotion and pain. The darkness that allows me to smile and mindlessly walk to complete these remedial tasks while hiding the fact that I can't afford to eat. Surely, this feeling is normal though. After all, this is how they taught me to be. Perhaps I should just open my eyes again, stop dreaming, and get back to work now.

Brainwashed

Brainwashed from a young age. Really from the moment you took your first breath. Constantly told how beautiful the world is. How great where you live is. How amazing your family is. How not only can you be anything but that you get whatever you set your heart on. Only to discover these are all lies. Lies slowly peeled away as you age and begin to taste the filth of your reality.

The very things you were promised will be revealed as bitter lies. This world will eat you, your hopes, and your dreams in a flash. Then before there's even time to mourn, life will be busy throwing these chewed-up dreams back at you in the form of regret as it laughs in your face.

It seems as though nothing is sacred. Those who are supposed to love and protect you are sometimes the very ones who destroy, corrupt, and harm you. The ones you so treasured turn out to be the ones burying you in filth. Those who you bring yourself close to are often those who cut you. And why shouldn't they? It's hard to miss with a knife when you stand next to your target.

We wake up hoping for direction and purpose. However, it seems as though we are only stumbling around and wandering aimlessly as we try to fill the void in our hearts. The void that was created by the falsehoods and illusions meant to serve as blinders to protect us from the truth. Did it work? Does anyone feel as though they are where they should be? Better yet, does anyone feel like they are where they want to be? Where that innocent child they once were told everyone what they would one day be? After being raised in a world of irony and contradictions, our reality becomes blurred. Forced to become inhuman machines to properly and cohesively live in a human society. A planet full of wonders and dreamers, yet the best we can do is ruin it and steal from each other. Misery loves company after all. We've been brainwashed from a young age.

Void

I find myself in between worlds and realities

I find myself in between time and space

I am neither here nor away

I am neither alive nor barely breathing

I am both lost in myself and found in my own truth

I am both surrounded by darkness and enveloped by light

I search for the answers that my brain and heart long for

I search for the love that I have thrown away and turned off again

My head sings both my victory songs and the tunes of my devils

My heart sings of my lust and of its own shattered form

I seek the truth, only to find lies

I seek my sanity, only to find emptiness

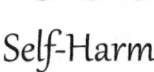

Self-Harm

The louder my world grows, the more I appreciate the silence in this life. The thunderous calamity of the world around me is deafening. The voices fill the air, shouting how bad you are, how weak you are, how stupid you are, how you're never enough. Fresh steel glides so easily though. Suddenly, all is quiet again. Even if only for a moment, at least the pain silences everything else.

The End

I've never been very sure on anything in my life
Yeah, it's a great height
But I want to be sure the rope is nice and tight
I don't know if the fall would kill me
Hopefully, the rope will catch me
My moment of bliss
A fleeting moment of freedom
To be flying through the air
To soar like a bird
Falling quickly
No worries
Only
To
Snap.
I created the rope with my own hands
How could it fail me?
Why have I been forsaken yet again?
I climb this bridge every day and jump
But nothing ever happens
I never feel any pain or joy
I simply want to feel something
I want to see myself swing
To see that I finally did one thing right
That I finally accomplished something

Is that too much to ask?
Maybe tomorrow will work
Maybe then I can find peace
Maybe then I can feel again
Or maybe I'm already dead.

An Easy Day

It's so easy. Fill your heart with hate. Set the world around you on fire, and the only thing you'll ever feel again is warmth. Warmth that you created. Isn't that grand? The pain fades. The screams stop. The suffering ends. Your light grows even bright around you. If this world was so cruel to you, then what right does it have to stop you? It's so easy, and it all starts with you.

What to Say

You've always got something else to say

Always asking someone else to pay

You never want to take responsibility

Just own up to your own shit show

You stay so high, will you ever come back down?

You drink so much I wonder when you'll drown

We're all a little fucked up

We're all a little crazy

That's what makes this so much fun

That's what makes me want to run

I don't really know what else to say

I just want this pain to go away

Torn between my own self-destruction

And reining chaos everywhere around me

Watching all I loved disappear

Watching all I earned disappear

I stay pissed off because I can't even keep up with those closest to me

Your gun was loaded, and you were ready to end it all, but I was nowhere to be found

My heart breaks, my heart aches

My soul left my body, my soul spits in my face

How could I have become such a sorry disgrace?

I smile and laugh to hide from those that are around me

To hide the fact that I hate everything about me and all that surrounds me

I kid, and I joke to make light of this darkness that grows within

They say I should get help, but I don't even know where to begin

I yell in my head because I'm too scared to say anything aloud

I yell at myself to do better to make myself proud

I swim in my head

I toss and turn in my bed

I don't really know what else to say

I just wish this pain would go away

Why can't I get the thoughts of you away?

You never really cared

So why can't I just walk away?

Why am I cursed to be stuck with you in my brain forever?

I walked out on the ones who cared

I turned away from every challenge

I'm so sick of being in this place

I can't even stand to look at my own face

I don't really know what else to say

I just wish this pain would go away.

Death and Dissonance

Death and dissonance. Disemboweled for your rhetoric. Dismemberment and destruction. Chaos and carnage surrounding your lives. Watch me gouge out their eyes. Eliminating all that is dear to you. Wreckage brought forth by your hands. Death to all that you love for the sake of money and profit. Spill the blood of the innocent. Their bodies pile on the streets. This is your life now. You're the one who let the corruption seed and sprout. You're the one who refused to stand and stop this evil. Now suffer in silence. Die while you beg for your pathetic existence to last a moment longer. Cry from your empty eye sockets, and bleed unto the tainted earth. Suffer for an eternity for the wrongs you left behind. Join the cycle of death and dissonance.

The Final Fight

Suicide, you or I, do or die
First to bleed will concede
Hate in your heart, murder is my art
Removed the head, now she's dead
Throw it away, get it away
Suffer in silence, embrace the violence
Drain the guts and drink the blood
Never more than total destruction of self and society
Watch them die like the rats they are
Ripping throats out, I silence the world
An eye for an eye was too kind
I'll watch you burn from my throne
Hang the heads, dismember the bodies
Watch my madness unfold
The evil within was untold
Tricked, tried, beaten, and abused
To you, it was a game, one big ruse
See my revenge, watch as I split their skulls
Hear my howl, taste my axe
Look into the eyes of nothing
Look into the eyes of hatred
I'll turn you to a pile of dust and bone
You did this, you brought this
Now suffer in silence, embrace my violence

End of You

Why don't you suffer in silence

While I gouge out your eyes

While I fuck your skull

Blow out your brains with a 12-gauge

Painting the walls with misery

Desecrate all that you love

Traumatize you for eternity

Destroy all that you hold dear

Disrupt your own thoughts into hating yourself?

Let me be clear

Suffer in silence

Break your own heart

Why. Won't. You. Just fucking die?

Robbery

Splatter and tatter

Bits to matter

Run it around and let it scatter.

Bold and fold

You should always do as you're told

Look at you now, growing cold.

Smash and bash

You should've given them all of your cash.

Instead, your head is spread

Your body lay on a bed

Looking kind of funny as you're awfully dead.

Hellhounds

I hate those dogs. Their stench is beyond foul. Their fur burnt mostly off and flesh half-cooked by the fire in their bellies. They stare and stare, waiting for you to move. Letting the fear build up inside before they run you down like a chew toy being thrown. Patiently looking at you, drooling. It's the same dream over and over again. Every night I see them, I become fully aware that I am in a dream, but I can never escape. The pain of being ripped apart after they chase me down is always so intense. I wake up in a sweat and shaking. Too afraid to go back to sleep. Too tired to stay awake. These dogs are killing me one restless night at a time. I enter the dream on the street of which I grew up on. Everything looks normal at first, but the clouds roll in quickly. The sky turns to a reddish hue. The once-pristine roads and houses are now crumbling. The beautiful green shrubbery now barren of all leaves and flowers. I face front to see them waiting yet again. Sometimes there are several, sometimes only two but always at least two. I know I have to move to get away. I must run to survive. But I realize there's no point because they always catch me. For years, I have been tormented by this. For years, I begged to understand, why me? Why must I suffer? When will it finally be my turn to have a peaceful night's sleep? I'll tie this rope off, and this will either be the last time those damn dogs torment me or the first time I sleep peacefully. The hounds from hell have won, and I'm too tired to care.

Reflection

With every step forward, I doubt

With every jump, I fear I will not reach the other side

While crawling through, I pity myself

With each waking moment, I am filled with terror.

No matter what I have accomplished

No matter how confident I seem

No matter how calm I look

Am I enough?

My Love

All the things I have done for you. The wars I started. The blood I spilt with my own hands. Everything that I crushed and destroyed for you. All you had to do was point. I would gladly do it again too. I wouldn't skip a beat or bat an eyelash for any request you presented me with. In my eyes, the world and everything on it belongs to you. Anyone who dare disagree is a poison that must be eradicated immediately. I'd take anything, make anything, or destroy everything with glee if that's what your heart so desired. All I wanted in return was a chance to look at you one more time. Each look sturdied my resolve and refilled my heart. No matter how dark and spiteful I become, I'll do it for you. It seems you don't want to look at me anymore. You don't want to see the monster I've turned in to. You despise me, and I don't blame you. I did everything to show my love for you. You never loved me back though. The only poison being eradicated was my sanity. The person I created out of my true self for your pleasure was being destroyed. Now this poor creature will spill blood for you one last time. I will do one last service to you as a symbol of the strength of what I had for you. I'll spill the blood of the creature you hate the most as I slit my own throat. For you.

Unnamed Friend

This little black cat has been my only constant in this world. He's my best friend, yet I don't even know his name. He came into my life four years ago, and now, not a day passes where we don't sit together each morning and evening. Dad is always working, and Mom is constantly running off. Whenever they are both home, all they do is fight. Sometimes, they remind me that I am the reason they fight and why they struggle so much. That I'm the reason they don't love each other anymore. I'm twelve now though. Finally old enough to start contributing to my family. At least that's what the other kids tell me. Maybe then, my parents will love me like this cat does. Maybe then I will be able to talk to them and live happily like I do in these brief moments with my friend. That's what I'm hoping for at least. The last thing I remember was sitting with my friend on the porch. Mom and Dad were yelling a lot. There was a loud bang. Another. Yet another. Then there were lights flashing around me. I feel hot. My friend is frantically meowing at me, but I can't get my hands to move to pet him. My hair feels wet. I can't hear what these people are yelling at me. I don't understand why they are all gathering around and crying. I feel so heavy and tired. I'll just take a quick nap. I hope someone can feed my friend. Maybe they could even help me finally pick a name for him. I'm just happy that my parents have finally stopped fighting. Now I can nap with my best friend in the sunshine. How nice.

www.ingramcontent.com/pod-product-compliance
Lightning Source LLC
Chambersburg PA
CBHW031434040426
42444CB00006B/806